Toes

Written by William Butland
Photography by Graham Meadows

Whose Toes Are These?

Look at these tracks.
Can you guess whose toes made them?

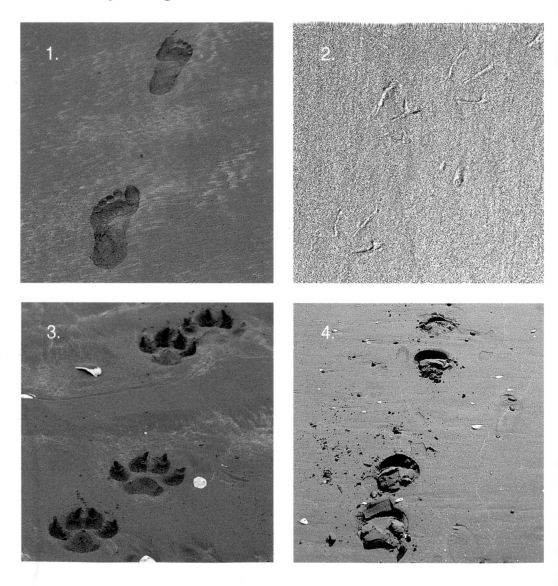

We can tell what animal
made the tracks by the shape
and size of the toe prints.

1. These tracks were
   made by a person.

2. These are the tracks
   of a bird.

3. These tracks were
   made by a dog.

4. A horse made
   these tracks.

3

People's Toes

Look at the toes on this foot.

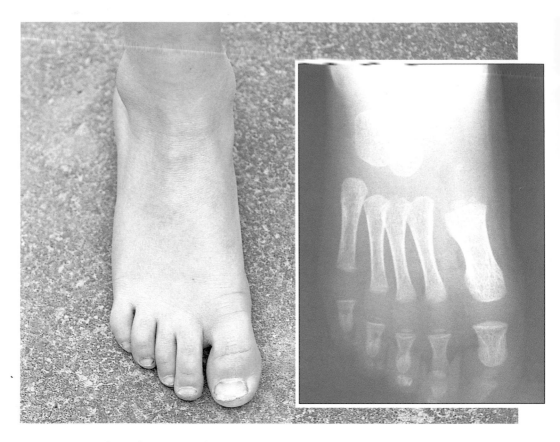

People have five toes on each foot.
On top of each toe is a toenail.
The big toe has two bones,
while the other toes each
have three bones.

4

What Are Toes For?

What do you use your toes for?
Stand with your feet flat on the floor
so that your toes and heels are
touching the ground.

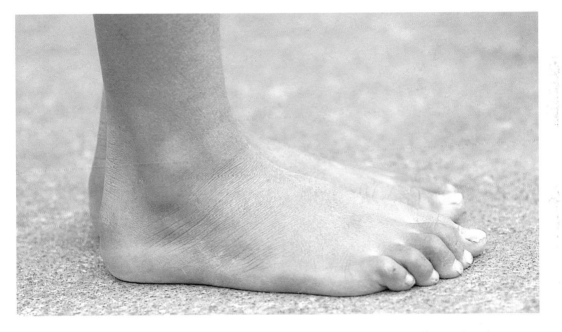

Now try to stand on just your heels.
It is very hard to keep your balance
without using your toes.
You use your toes to help you keep
your balance.

You also use your toes
to help you move.
Walk a few steps in your bare feet.
In these photographs, see how the toes
on one foot push off the ground
as the other foot swings forward
to take a step.

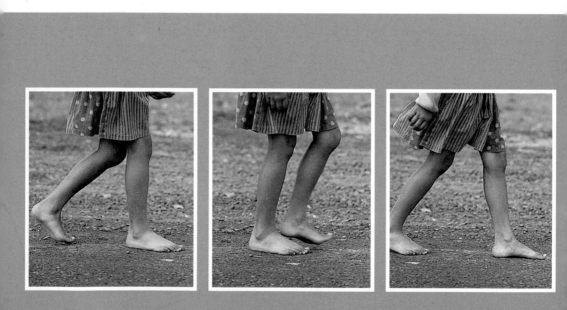

When you run, you use your toes
even more.

Try to stand on your tiptoes.

It is very hard to stay up
on your tiptoes for a long time.
Ballet dancers wear special shoes
so that they can dance on the very
tips of their toes.

Animals such as birds, cats, and horses also use their toes to help them move.

Toes for Walking

Some animals walk on
the tips of their toes.
Animals that have hoofs to protect
their toes are called ungulates.
Hoofs are special hard coverings
that grow around the animals' toes.

Horses, pigs, and cows, like this one, are all ungulates.

Many ungulates have
an even number of toes.
Other ungulates have
an odd number of toes.

The rhinoceros has three toes on each foot.

What other animals walk on their toes?

Elephants walk on their toes.

Cats and dogs also walk on their toes.

Not all animals walk on their toes.
Some animals, such as bears
and badgers, walk with the whole foot
touching the ground.
People also walk like this.

Polar bears walk with their feet flat on the ground.

Toenails and Claws

Many animals have toe coverings similar to toenails. Elephants have toes, but they are hidden. The only way you can find an elephant's toes is by looking for its toe coverings.

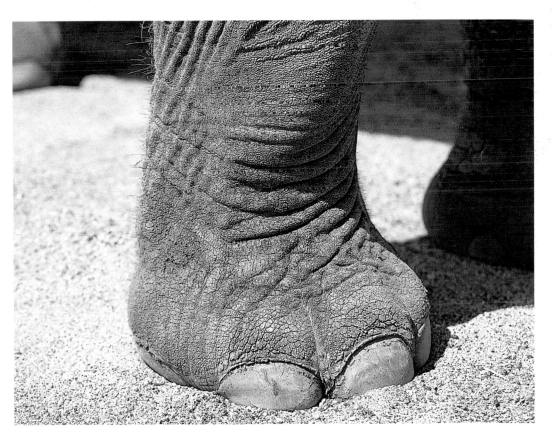

Some animals, such as kangaroos,
pandas, and squirrels, have claws
on the ends of their toes. Each claw
curves around the last toe bone.

Can you tell what animal
these claws belong to?

These claws belong to a dog.

A cat can pull its claws in
when they are not needed.
This helps keep them sharp.

Toe Pads

Many animals have special cushions under their toes called toe pads.

Toe pads help protect the animal's toes from the hard ground.

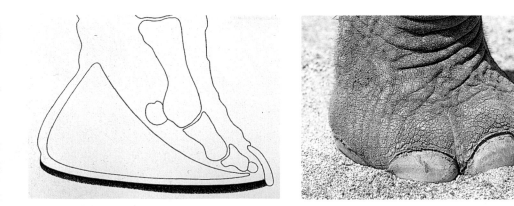

The elephant has a large pad that surrounds its toes.

The camel has a large toe pad
on the end of its toes.
The pad helps the camel to walk
on the soft surface of the desert sand.

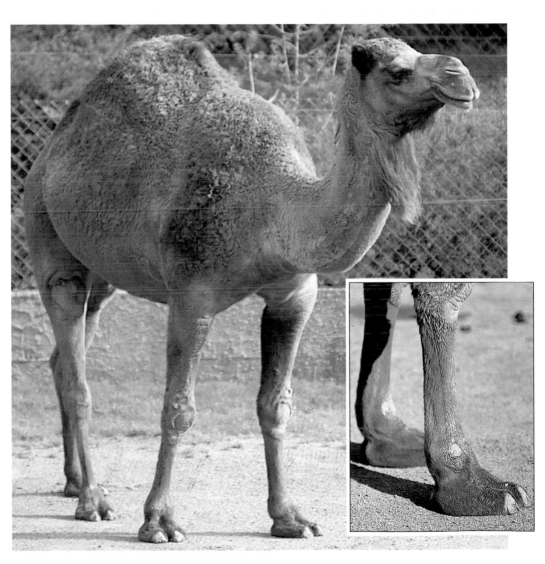

Birds and Their Toes

Birds also use their toes
to help them move or stand.

The emu, which cannot fly, moves by running and walking on its long legs and strong toes.

The brolga crane wades in water. It has long, spread-out toes, which keep it from sinking in the soft mud.

Birds that sit, or perch, on branches have three front toes and one back toe on each foot.

This myna is using its toes to hold on to a tree branch.

Perching birds can even lock their toes around a branch so that they won't fall off when they are asleep.

Toes for Swimming

Some animals use their toes
to help them swim.
Many birds that swim, such as ducks,
penguins, and sea gulls, have toes
that are joined together by skin.
These webbed feet help the birds swim.

This goose can use its webbed feet to paddle.

Many other animals that swim
also have webbed feet.

This frog has webbed feet.

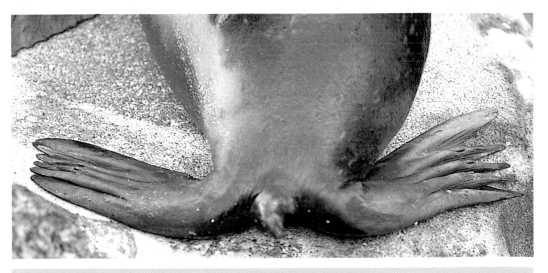

This sea lion also has webbed feet.

Other Uses for Toes

Toes can be used to do many things.
Can you hold something
between your toes?
Many animals can.
Chimpanzees and orangutans can
use their big toes like a thumb.

A chimpanzee

Some animals use their toes
to scratch and groom themselves.

Geckos use their toes
to climb smooth surfaces.

This forest gecko has special suction pads on each
toe that help it walk upside down.

Toes can be used for many things.

Toes can be used for moving.

Toes can be used for
holding on to things.

Toes can be used
for digging.

Toes are very important.